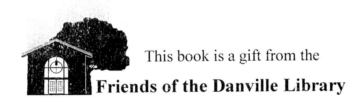

Bugs That Help

Kirsten Weir

 **Marshall Cavendish**
Benchmark

New York

Marshall Cavendish Benchmark
99 White Plains Road
Tarrytown, NY 10591
www.marshallcavendish.us

All Internet addresses were available and accurate when this book was sent to press.

Library of Congress Cataloging-in-Publication Data

Weir, Kirsten.
    Bugs that help / by Kirsten Weir.
    p. cm. -- (Bug alert)
    Includes bibliographical references and index.
    ISBN 978-0-7614-3192-3
1. Beneficial insects--Juvenile literature. 2. Insects--Juvenile literature. I. Title.
    SF517.W39 2009
    595.716'3--dc22
    2008014598

The photographs in this book are used by permission and through the courtesy of:

Half Title : Digitalife/ Shutterstock
Troy Casswell/ Shutterstock : P4 ; Anna Chelnokova/ Shutterstock : P5 ;
alle/ Shutterstock : P6 tr ; SCOTT CAMAZINE / SCIENCE PHOTO LIBRARY : P7 ; vnlit/ Shutterstock : P8 tr ; Borut Gorenjak/ Shutterstock : P9 ; Digitalife/ Shutterstock : P10 tr ; Ronald Caswell/ Shutterstock : P11 ; Adam Gryko/ Shutterstock : P12 tr ; JACK CLARK/ Animals Animals/ Photolibrary : P13 ; Eric Isselée/ Shutterstock : P14 tr ; Cathy Keifer/ Bigstockphoto : P15 ; Papilio / Alamy : P16 ; STEVE GSCHMEISSNER / SCIENCE PHOTO LIBRARY : P19 ; KONRAD WOTHE / MINDEN PICTURES : P21 ; Oxford Scientific / Photolibrary : P23 ; NATURE'S IMAGES / SCIENCE PHOTO LIBRARY : P25 ; Mircea BEZERGHEANU/ Shutterstock : P26 tr ; MARTIN DOHRN / SCIENCE PHOTO LIBRARY : P27 ; VOLKER STEGER / SCIENCE PHOTO LIBRARY : P29.

Cover photo: Erich Kuchling/ Picture Press/ Photolibrary

Illustrations : Q2A Media Art Bank

Created by: Q2A Media

Creative Director: Simmi Sikka

Series Editor: Maura Christopher

Series Art Director: Sudakshina Basu

Series Designers: Mansi Mittal, Rati Mathur and Shruti Bahl

Series Illustrators: Indranil Ganguly, Rishi Bhardwaj, Kusum Kala and Pooja Shukla

Photo research by Anju Pathak

Series Project Managers: Ravneet Kaur and Shekhar Kapur

Printed in Malaysia

135642

Contents

Little Helpers

Millions of different kinds of bugs roam Earth. They include insects, worms, and other wiggly little invertebrates. Invertebrates are animals without backbones. They have big roles to play. Some bugs are food for bigger animals. Other bugs help break down decaying plants and animals, returning minerals from them to the soil. Without help from these bugs, new plants would not have the nutrients they need to grow.

Bugs help people in more specific ways, too. Some bugs are useful in medicine. Many bugs help in gardens and on farms. Some eat other bugs that munch on crops. Other bugs lend a helping wing by **pollinating** flowers and trees. Plants must be pollinated to grow seeds and fruit. Bugs help those plants survive.

One Bug, Two Bug

Two kinds of bugs are especially helpful to people:

Insects. Adult insects have six legs and are the type of bug most familiar to us. They usually have wings. These insects help us by pollinating plants, eating garden pests, and making products, such as honey, that are useful to people.

Worms. All worms—from earthworms to leeches—lack arms and legs. They get around by wiggling. Worms are important to the **ecosystem**. They help the world by keeping the soil healthy for plants and other animals. Leeches are helpful in a weirder way. Doctors sometimes use them to help people heal!

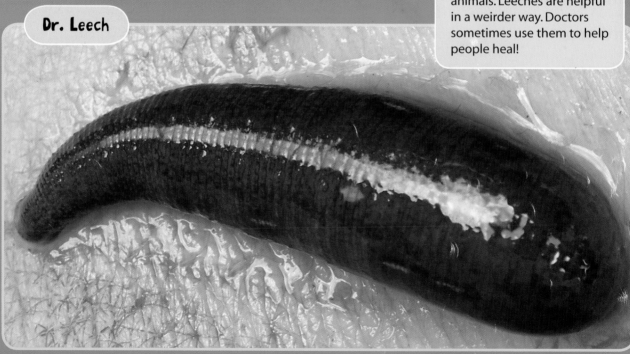

Dr. Leech

Butterfly wings are covered in tiny, colorful scales.

Butterflies sense their surroundings with a pair of antennae.

Butterflies help out by pollinating plants. They spread pollen so that flowers and trees can grow seeds and fruit.

Honeybees

Honeybees are hard-working bugs. They make honey and beeswax.

◄ A typical beehive can contain more than 50,000 bees!

What Are They?

Honeybees are insects. They live together in large groups called **colonies**. Each honeybee colony contains one queen bee, which lays eggs. The other females in the colony are workers. They take care of young bees, keep the hive clean, and guard it. They also leave the hive to collect food. The only job of the male drone is to mate with the queen.

Thanks, Honey!

Worker bees collect **pollen** and **nectar** from flowers. Back at the hive, the workers make the nectar into honey. One hive of honeybees can produce 80 pounds (36 kilograms) of honey each year. Bees also make a substance called beeswax, which is used in candles.

Life Cycle

1. The queen bee lays all the eggs in the colony.
2. Worker bees move each egg to its own hole inside the honeycomb.
3. After the eggs hatch, worker bees feed pollen and honey to the **larvae** (young bees).
4. As adults, bees leave the honeycomb to join the rest of the hive.
5. When the queen bee dies, one of the female worker bees will replace her and start laying eggs.

Life Cycle

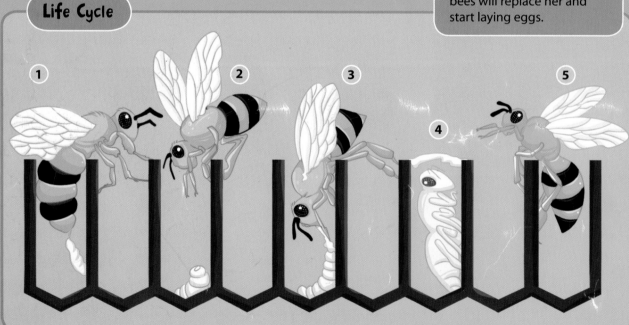

Honeybees use chemicals to communicate with other members of the hive.

Bees see through five eyes. Two large eyes perceive shape and color. Three smaller eyes see only light and dark. They cannot see the color red.

Bees have six legs and two pairs of wings. They can buzz through the air at 20 miles (32 kilometers) per hour.

Bees' bodies are divided into three segments.

One queen lays all the eggs for the colony. A queen can lay 2,000 eggs in a single day!

Female honeybees have stingers on their rears. Bees sting to protect the hive. When a honeybee stings an animal or person, her stinger breaks off and she dies.

Bees

Bees are important pollinators. They help plants grow by carrying pollen from flower to flower.

What Are They?

Bees are insects. About 3,500 different kinds of bees live in North America alone! Like honeybees, some live together in large colonies. Most bees, however, do not live in groups.

Busy Bees

Female bees lay their eggs in nests on the ground, in trees, or in hives that they build. Bees feed on nectar and pollen from flowers. They also bring back pollen to their nests to feed the baby bees.

When a bee visits a flower to feed, grains of pollen stick to the hairs on its body. At the next flower it visits, some of the pollen falls off, pollinating the flower. The plant can then produce fruits. Bees pollinate more than one hundred different crops in the United States, including almonds, apples, blueberries, cherries, cucumbers, sunflowers, and watermelons.

▲ Only female bees can sting!

What Is Pollination?

Many plants cannot make seeds unless they receive pollen from another plant. Without new seeds, there would be no new plants. Luckily, bugs offer plants a helping hand. By carrying pollen from flower to flower, bugs like bees make sure plants get the pollen they need to survive.

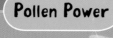

Pollen Power

Many fruit and vegetable crops would not grow without bees to pollinate them. Some farmers even borrow bee colonies from beekeepers so the farmers can pollinate their crops.

Instead of bones, bees have a hard outer shell called an exoskeleton.

Bees have fuzzy bodies. Pollen sticks to the fuzz and is transferred from flower to flower.

Bees have six legs and two pairs of wings. They can fly 15 to 20 miles (24 to 32 km) per hour.

Bees "smell" using antennae on their heads.

The sacks on bees' hind legs are called pollen baskets. They use the baskets to carry pollen from flowers to the hive.

Butterflies

Caterpillars, which are baby butterflies, can be pests. They eat the leaves off plants. They grow up to help, though. Adult butterflies pollinate many kinds of flowers.

What Are They?

Like all insects, butterflies have six legs. Covered with tiny scales, their two large pairs of wings are often very colorful. When you touch a butterfly, the scales may come off on your fingers, like colorful dust.

They Like It Bright

Butterflies visit many wildflowers in search of nectar to drink. Many flowers smell like perfume to attract bugs to pollinate them. Butterflies have a poor sense of smell, so flowers cannot attract them with odor. Butterflies do have great eyesight, however, and are attracted to brightly colored flowers. Their favorites are flowers that grow in clusters or clumps, which make a good platform for them to land on.

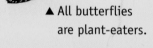

▲ All butterflies are plant-eaters.

Life Cycle

1 A butterfly egg hatches, and a caterpillar emerges.
2 The caterpillar feeds on leaves and other plant parts.
3 When the caterpillar is large enough, it spins a **cocoon** of silk around itself.
4 The caterpillar grows wings and develops into an adult inside the cocoon. The butterfly emerges from the cocoon and spreads out its new wings.

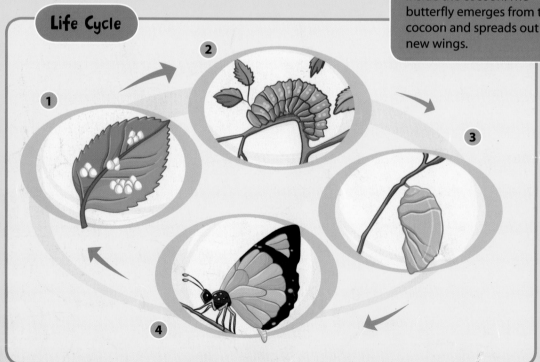

Life Cycle

Some butterflies have special "ears." The ears help them listen for bats, animals that like to snack on butterflies.

Butterflies have large eyes and good vision. Unlike bees, butterflies can see the color red as well as many other colors.

Butterflies taste with their feet.

Butterflies drink nectar through long, skinny, tubelike tongues. When they are not eating, butterflies roll up their tongues so they don't get in the way.

Ladybugs

Is something snacking on your vegetable garden? Call in the ladybugs! These familiar polka-dotted bugs help out by eating common garden pests.

What Are They?

Ladybugs are a type of insect known as a beetle. Beetles have two pairs of wings. They use the inner pair of wings for flying. The outer wings are hard, forming a protective shell around the bug. The shiny, round bugs are usually bright red or orange, with black spots.

Big Appetites

Ladybugs have big appetites for **aphids**, small insects that are common garden pests. Ladybugs are **predators**, feeding on aphids and other pesky bugs. Adult ladybugs can eat as many as seventy-five aphids in a single day!

There are 4,000 ▶ kinds of ladybugs around the world.

Life Cycle

1. Adult ladybugs lay clusters of eggs inside colonies of aphids.

2. The eggs hatch five days later, and the larvae feed on the aphids.

3. After two or three weeks, the larvae form **pupae**, or protective cases, around their bodies.

4. A week or so later, adult ladybugs emerge from the pupae. In summer, female ladybugs start laying eggs. In autumn, they find a safe place to spend the winter. When spring arrives, the ladybugs will leave their winter hiding spots to lay more eggs.

Life Cycle

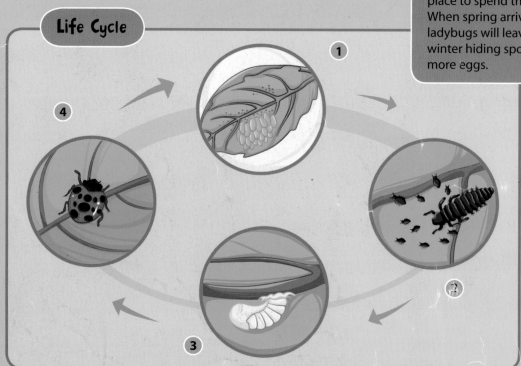

Ladybugs have powerful jaws for attacking aphids.

A hard, dome-shaped shell covers a ladybug. The shell is made of the bug's outer wings. Tucked under these hard outer wings is a thin pair of wings for flying.

In some places, ladybugs are called lady beetles or lady bird beetles.

Ladybugs have six legs.

Their red and black coloring warns birds that the bugs do not taste good.

Praying Mantises

Praying mantises are named for the way they hold their long front legs. They fold their legs in front of them as though they are praying.

What Are They?

Praying mantises are insects. Fierce predators, mantises help in the garden by feasting on bugs that damage plants. Their long front legs are designed for catching bugs. Sharp spines on their legs help them catch their **prey**. Mantises are usually brown or green. These colors help them blend into their surroundings. They sit perfectly still, waiting for a bug to wander nearby. Then, in an instant—they strike!

Dangerous Relationships

Many people think that the female praying mantis bites the head off the male after they mate! Actually, the males often escape unharmed.

▲ Mantises have wings but are clumsy fliers.

Life Cycle

1. In the fall, a female mantis seals her eggs inside a hard case. She attaches the case to a tree branch.
2. In the spring, **nymphs** hatch from the eggs. They look like tiny adult mantises without wings.
3. The nymphs feed and grow throughout the summer. Each time they **molt**, or shed their skin, they grow larger.
4. Finally, they grow wings and become adults. In the fall, the adults will lay more eggs.

Life Cycle

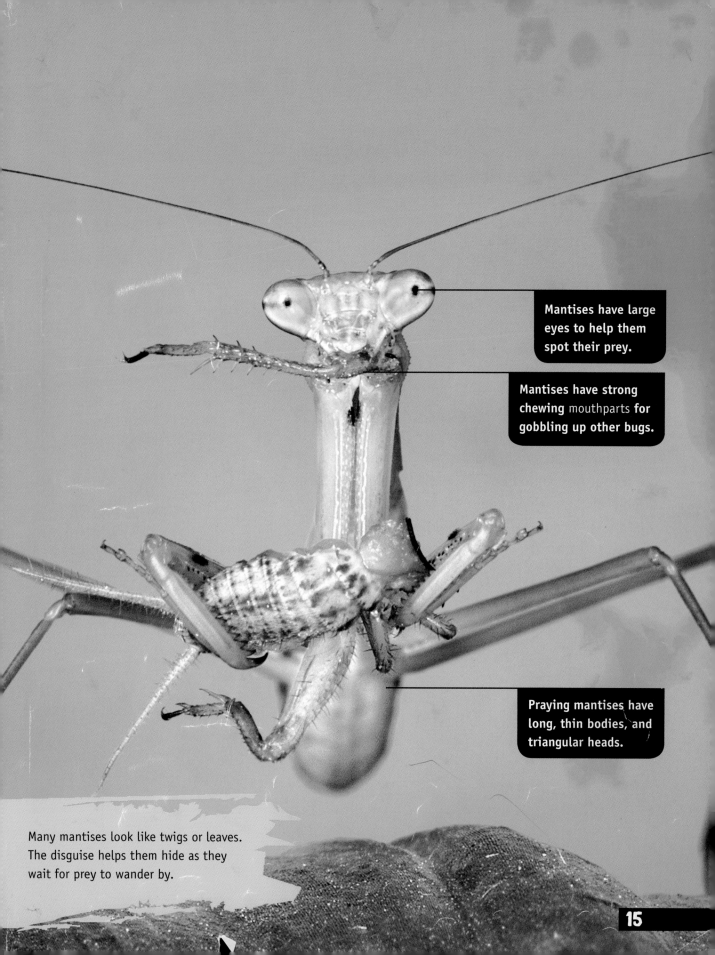

Mantises have large eyes to help them spot their prey.

Mantises have strong **chewing** mouthparts **for gobbling up other bugs.**

Praying mantises have long, thin bodies, and triangular heads.

Many mantises look like twigs or leaves. The disguise helps them hide as they wait for prey to wander by.

Green Lacewings

Lacewings are pretty, delicate-looking bugs, but looks can be deceiving! Lacewing babies are fierce predators.

What Are They?

Green lacewings are insects. They have six legs and two pairs of wings. Adults are about 1 inch (2.5 centimeters) long, with lime green bodies and yellow heads.

▲ Adult lacewings are slow fliers.

Little Lions

Adult lacewings usually feed on nectar and pollen. Their larvae, though, are excellent hunters and look like tiny alligators! They especially like to eat aphids. Aphids are small bugs that can destroy fruits and vegetables. Lacewing larvae eat so many aphids, in fact, that they are sometimes called aphid lions. One baby lacewing can gobble up to two hundred pest bugs in one week. Some gardeners and farmers even buy boxes of lacewing eggs to release into their fields!

Life Cycle

1. A female lacewing can lay more than two hundred eggs in her lifetime. Each egg is perched atop a long, hairlike stalk.
2. When the eggs hatch, the young feed on aphids and other garden pests.
3. After two or three weeks, the larvae spin silk pupae (cocoons) around their bodies.
4. After five days, adults lacewings hatch.

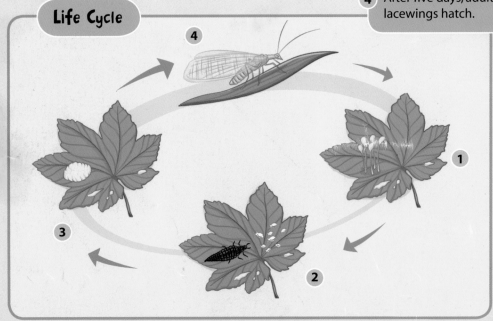

Life Cycle

Adult lacewings have four large, see-through wings. Veins crisscross their wings, making them look like delicate lace.

The young bugs are covered with bristles.

Lacewings sense their surroundings with a pair of long antennae.

Lacewings see through a pair of large eyes.

Baby lacewings have strong jaws for eating aphids and other bugs.

Lacewing babies have no wings.

European Weevils

The weevil's face ends in a long, curved snout like an elephant's trunk. This weird-looking bug is helping to save wild places from unwelcome plants.

What Are They?

Weevils are a type of insect known as beetles. Beetles are some of the most common bugs on the planet. The European weevil is dark brown, with little tufts of white hairs on its body.

◄ These weevils can spend their whole lives on purple loosestrife plants.

Purple Plant Eater

Some European weevils have been let loose in the United States to help control a weed called purple loosestrife. This weed grows out of control. It takes over wetlands, killing other plants and destroying marshes. Fortunately, the European weevil has a taste for this nasty plant. Scientists and park rangers have released millions of the hungry bugs across the country. They gobble up the purple loosestrife but not other plants. Thanks to the weevils, wetlands are becoming healthy once again.

Life Cycle

1. An adult weevil lays her eggs on purple loosestrife plants.
2. When the eggs hatch, the larvae burrow into the plant and feed on its roots.
3. After one or two years, they form pupae inside the roots of the plant.
4. Adults emerge from the pupae. They start feeding on purple loosestrife leaves.

Life Cycle

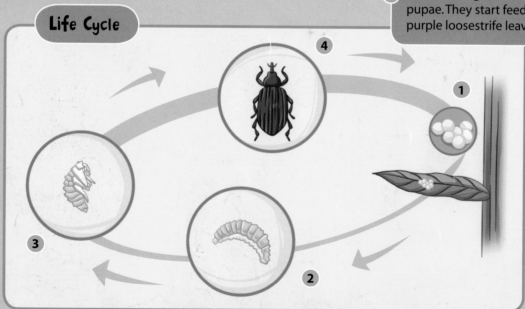

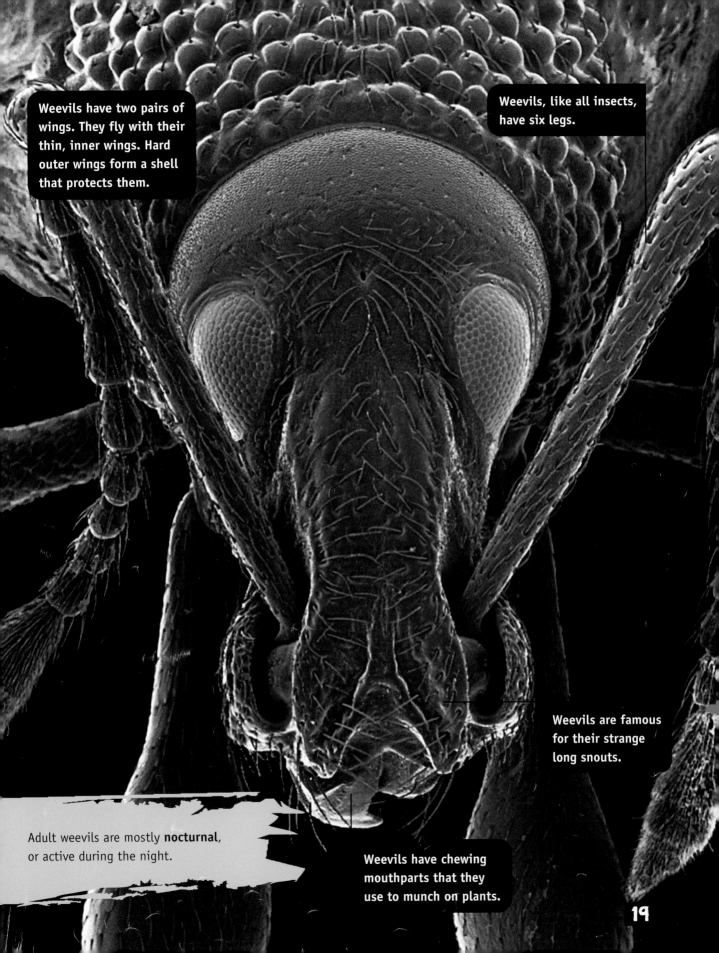

Weevils have two pairs of wings. They fly with their thin, inner wings. Hard outer wings form a shell that protects them.

Weevils, like all insects, have six legs.

Weevils are famous for their strange long snouts.

Adult weevils are mostly **nocturnal**, or active during the night.

Weevils have chewing mouthparts that they use to munch on plants.

Earthworms

Many earthworms are barely 1 inch (2.5 cm) long, but some tropical worms can grow to 11 feet (3.3 meters)! Big or small, earthworms all play an important role in their ecosystem.

What Are They?

Earthworms are the most famous members of a group of animals called worms. Their thin, tubelike bodies are divided into many segments. That long, stretchy body is perfectly designed for tunneling underground.

Tunnel Builders

Earthworms tunnel through the dirt, creating channels that air and water can move through. These channels help plants and other bugs that live in the soil get the air and water that they need to survive. Worm droppings, called **castings**, are also rich in minerals. Minerals help plants and other bugs grow strong and healthy.

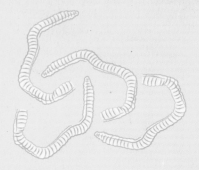

▲ Every earthworm has both male and female parts.

Life Cycle

1. Adult earthworms lay a cocoon full of eggs in the soil. The cocoon protects the eggs.
2. Baby worms hatch from the cocoon.
3. The young worms grow larger as they feed on bits of plants in the soil
4. When fully grown, adult earthworms release eggs of their own. Some earthworm species can live to be ten years old.

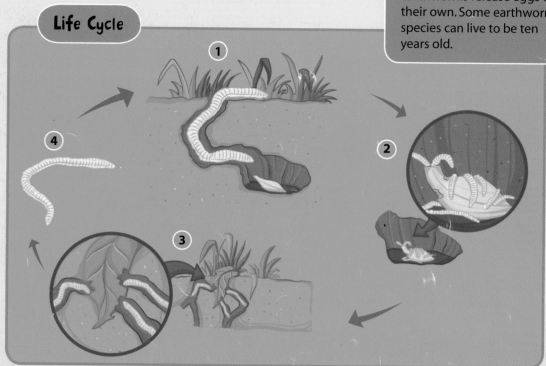

Life Cycle

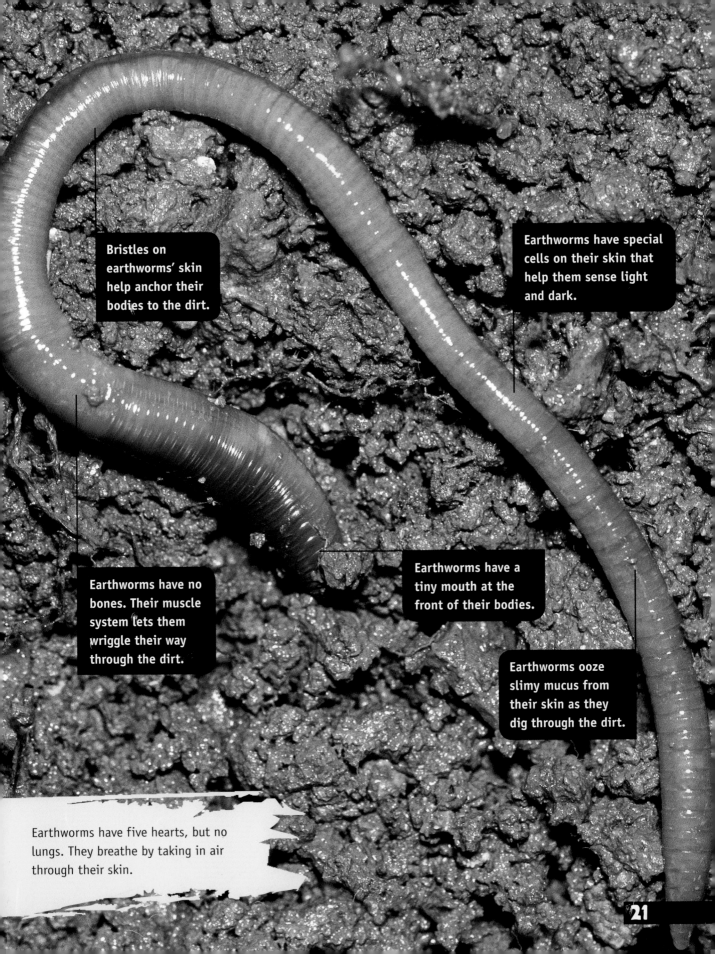

Bristles on earthworms' skin help anchor their bodies to the dirt.

Earthworms have special cells on their skin that help them sense light and dark.

Earthworms have no bones. Their muscle system lets them wriggle their way through the dirt.

Earthworms have a tiny mouth at the front of their bodies.

Earthworms ooze slimy mucus from their skin as they dig through the dirt.

Earthworms have five hearts, but no lungs. They breathe by taking in air through their skin.

Silkworms

Silkworms produce soft silk thread that people make into fabrics. Silkworm threads were first collected in China thousands of years ago.

What Are They?

Silkworms are not really worms. They are caterpillars! Silkworms are the immature form of furry white moths. Adult silk moths do not eat. Their caterpillars, however, eat constantly. After a month of eating and growing, they spin cocoons from silk that they make inside their bodies.

▲ Each year, silkworms produce enough silk to stretch from the Earth to the Sun six hundred times!

Shiny and Smooth

Each silkworm's cocoon is made from a single long piece of silk. The silken thread from one cocoon can stretch 3,000 feet (914 m)! People collect that thread to weave into fabrics. Silk is shiny and smooth—and expensive. It takes up to 3,000 cocoons to make just 1 pound (.45 kg) of silk fabric!

Life Cycle

1. Adult silk moths lay eggs that hatch into tiny caterpillars called silkworms.
2. The silkworms must eat within hours of hatching, or they will die. The caterpillars grow larger and larger.
3. As the caterpillars grow, they shed their skin. After shedding their skin four times, they spin cocoons of silk.
4. Two weeks later, adult moths hatch from the cocoon.

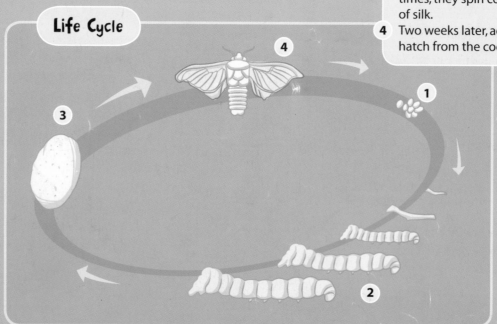

Life Cycle

As silkworms get bigger, a bulge grows behind their heads. The bulge is filled with silk. The silkworm uses this silk to spin its cocoon.

Silkworm caterpillars breathe through tiny holes in their bodies.

Their mouthparts are perfect for chewing leaves.

Silkworms will increase their body size 10,000 times during the month they spend as caterpillars!

Silkworms are white and often have black markings behind their heads.

Cochineal Insects

You may have never heard of this bug, but you have probably eaten parts of it! Cochineal insects produce a red dye used to color cloth, makeup, and even foods.

What Are They?

The cochineal insect is a scale insect. Scale insects suck the juices from plants. Cochineal insects spend their entire lives on cactus plants. The insects produce a bright red acid. This liquid makes them taste bad to predator bugs. Hundreds of years ago, the Aztec and Maya peoples of Central America discovered they could use the bugs to dye blankets and other fabrics.

▲ Male cochineal insects have wings, but females do not.

Seeing Red

Today, people still grind up the colorful cochineal insects to make natural dye called **carmine**. The dye is used to color food, fabric, and cosmetics. Carmine is all natural and safer than some chemical colorings.

Life Cycle

1 Cochineal insects lay eggs on cactus plants.
2 Young insects, called nymphs, hatch from the eggs.
3 The nymphs crawl to the edge of the cactus. Winds blow the tiny bugs to new cactus plants.
4 The insects feed on new cactus plants and develop into adults.

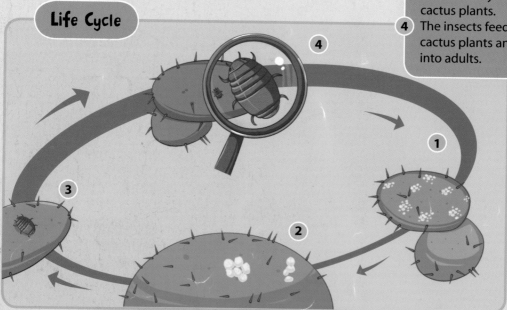

Life Cycle

Cochineal insects have small, soft, flat bodies

Cochineal insects are tiny, about 1/5 inches (5 millimeters) long.

Adult cochineal insects produce white clumps of material like cotton. The nymphs hide under the masses.

Cochineal insects have beaklike mouthparts. They use these mouthparts to suck juices from cactus plants.

Leeches

People have been using bloodsucking leeches in medicine for more than 2,000 years. Ancient doctors believed the slimy worms could heal wounds and ease fevers.

What Are They?

Leeches are worms. Though they have no legs or arms, they do have a mouth full of tiny, sharp teeth. Leeches normally live in lakes, rivers, and streams. They bite animals and suck their blood. The animals feel no pain.

▲ Mother leeches protect their young until the babies are old enough to care for themselves.

Now Hear This

When they bite, leeches inject a chemical into the open wound. The chemical keeps blood flowing, stopping the wound from forming a scab. Today, doctors sometimes use leeches to help patients after surgery. For example, a dog recently bit off a boy's ear. Doctors sewed the boy's ear back on and then stuck hungry leeches to his ear. The leeches kept blood flowing through the ear until the **blood vessels** inside had time to heal.

Life Cycle

1. A leech lays a mass of eggs inside a cocoon.
2. After about two weeks, the eggs hatch.
3. The baby leeches travel into the water of a stream or lake. There, they feed by sucking the blood of other animals.
4. When the young leeches grow into adults, they lay eggs of their own.

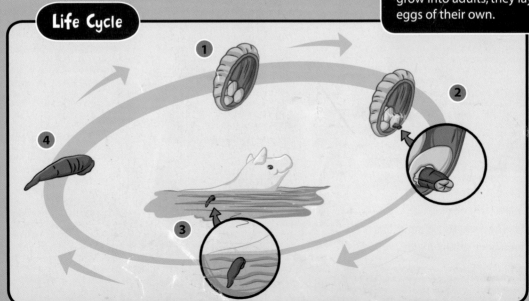

Life Cycle

26

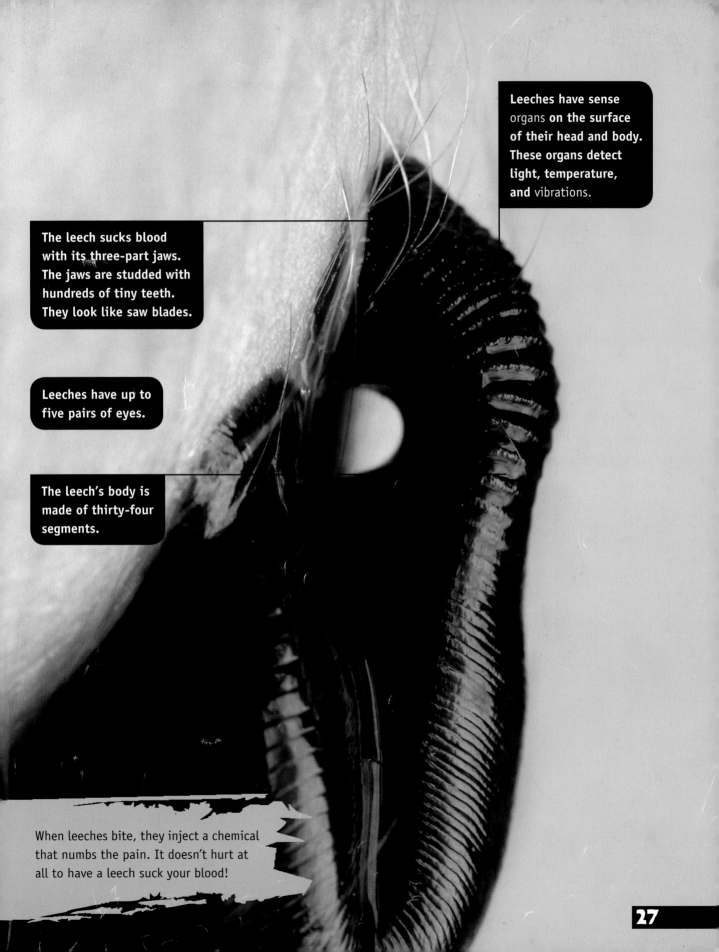

Leeches have sense organs **on the surface of their head and body. These organs detect light, temperature, and** vibrations.

The leech sucks blood with its three-part jaws. The jaws are studded with hundreds of tiny teeth. They look like saw blades.

Leeches have up to five pairs of eyes.

The leech's body is made of thirty-four segments.

When leeches bite, they inject a chemical that numbs the pain. It doesn't hurt at all to have a leech suck your blood!

Maggots

White, wriggling maggots look disgusting, but the tiny fly larvae are actually helpful. Some doctors rely on the bugs to help them treat patients with serious wounds.

What Are They?

Maggots are the larvae of flies. Wingless, legless, and toothless, maggots can only eat liquids. They spit a substance onto their food that makes it melt. Then the maggots suck up the liquid food with their tubelike mouthparts.

Wiggling in Wounds

Sometimes people have wounds that do not heal for months. Doctors sometimes place maggots inside the wound, where the maggots eat all the dead tissue. They also eat bacteria that might be infecting the sore. The maggots leave the healthy tissue alone.

▲ Maggots only eat dead tissue. They won't eat healthy, living flesh.

Life Cycle

1. An adult fly lays eggs on a rotting plant or animal.
2. The eggs hatch into larvae called maggots. They immediately begin feeding on the rotting tissue.
3. The maggots eat and grow.
4. Then they move to a dry place, such as the ground.
5. There, they form pupae. Inside the pupae, the maggots develop into adult flies.
6. After one or two weeks, adult flies emerge from the pupae.

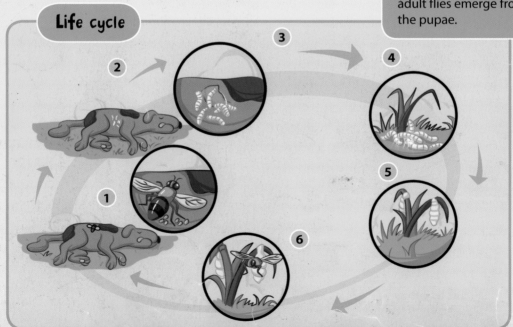

Life cycle

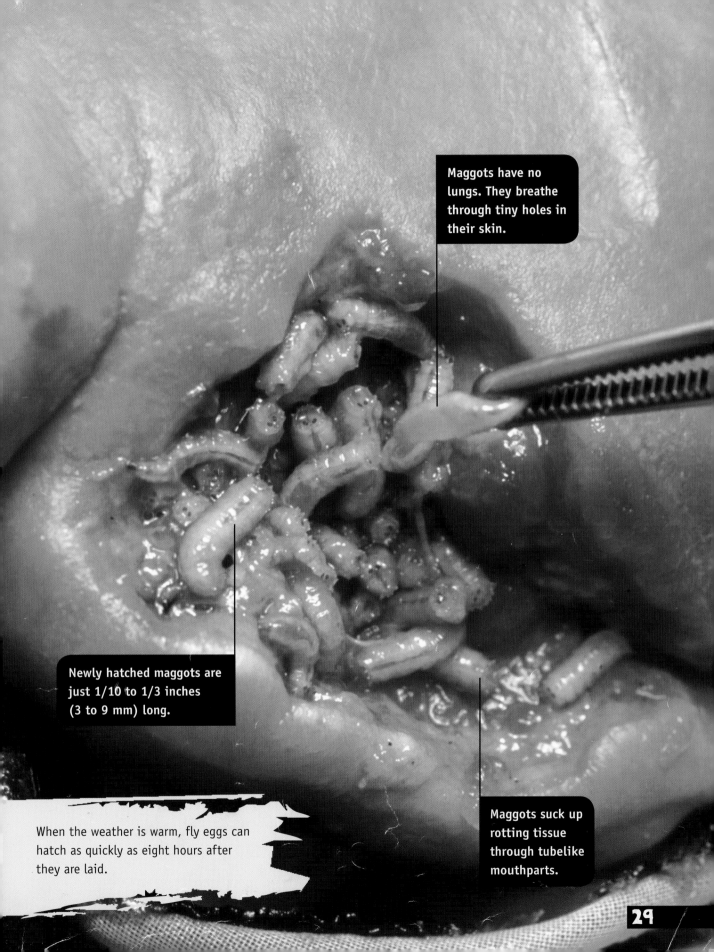

Maggots have no lungs. They breathe through tiny holes in their skin.

Newly hatched maggots are just 1/10 to 1/3 inches (3 to 9 mm) long.

When the weather is warm, fly eggs can hatch as quickly as eight hours after they are laid.

Maggots suck up rotting tissue through tubelike mouthparts.

Bugs Data

Books

Brust, Beth Wagner. *Butterflies*. San Diego, CA: Wildlife Education Ltd., 2000.

Kalmann, Bobbie. *The Life Cycle of an Earthworm*. Saint Catharines, Ontario: Crabtree Publishing Company, 2000.

Kite, Patricia L. *Leeches*. Minneapolis, MN: Lerner Publications, 2004.

Nichols, Catherine, ed. *Animal Planet: The Most Extreme Bugs*. San Francisco: Jossey-Bass, 2007.

O'Neill, Amanda. *Curious Kids Guides: Insects and Bugs*. London: Kingfisher Publications, 2002.

Winner, Cherie. *Everything Bug: What Kids Really Want to Know about Bugs*. Minocqua, WI: NorthWord Press, 2004.

Internet Sites

Visit these Web sites for more information:

Insectarium: An All Bug Museum
http://www.insectarium.com/insectarium.htm

PBS NOVA: *Tales from the Hive*
http://www.pbs.org/wgbh/nova/bees

Glossary

antenna (plural: antennae): A feeler located on the head of insects and other bugs.

aphid: A tiny insect that can destroy food crops and garden plants.

beeswax: A waxy substance made by bees that people use to make candles and makeup.

blood vessel: A tube that carries blood through the body.

carmine: A red dye made from the bodies of the cochineal insect.

castings: Earthworm dung.

cocoon: A covering usually made of silk threads that the larvae of some insects form around themselves. There, they pass the pupa stage.

colony: A group of animals, such as honeybees, that live together.

ecosystem: A community of plants and animals and the environment in which they live.

exoskeleton: The hard outer covering around the bodies of insects and other bugs.

invertebrate: An animal without a backbone.

larva (plural: larvae): The immature form of an insect.

molt: To shed the skin to grow into an adult form.

nectar: A sweet liquid produced by plants and eaten by many insects.

nocturnal: Active at night instead of during the day.

nutrient: A substance that living things need in order to grow and thrive.

nymph: An immature form of an insect. Nymphs are usually more developed than larvae.

organ: A part of the body that does a specific job, such as the heart, lungs, or stomach.

pollen: A powdery substance produced by plants in order to reproduce; many bugs eat pollen.

pollinate: To transfer pollen from flower to flower so that the plant can grow seeds and create new plants.

predator: An animal that eats other animals.

prey: An animal that is eaten by other animals.

pupa (plural: pupae): A cocoonlike resting form of an insect; the insect changes from an immature form to an adult form inside the pupa.

tropical: Having to do with the Tropics, a warm region of Earth that is near the equator.

vibrations: Tiny movements back and forth or up and down.

Index